Train of Thought

Poems from the Red Line

Jason Wright

To the dreamer in a nightmare.

another

publication

Published by Oddball Magazine Publishing
ISBN 9781733999809
Photography and Cover design by T.J. Edson
All Rights Reserved © 2019
Library of Congress Control Number: 2019940271

Stops

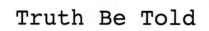

Truth Be Told

Every poem in this book, was written on the Red Line of the MBTA transit system in Boston, Massachusetts. Most, if not all, were written while in an anxiety-induced state, between the years 2011 and 2012.

Strap in.

NORTH QUINCY

Renaissance of Thought

Welcome to the Renaissance of Thought,

where the festival begins, and people dance
and talk.

Where the beautiful mix with
the ugly,

the poor with the rich,
the stoned with the sober,

the drunk with the rest.

This is a celebration
of tattoos
and bruises.

Love and Longing.

A drama and a comedy—
a theatrical production of *Macbeth*—

This: is the beginning—
a new bloom breathing.

This: is a dream—
between subway trains to find
peace through pain,

to teach myself restraint, honesty, and regret.

This: is the 11th inning in game 7 of a 7-game stretch.

This: is the Renaissance–
a new thought process.

The best medicine for me,

is this pen I am holding
and this notebook I am writing in.

I am entitling it:

Truth Be Told

No more lies here folks. It's time to rewind back to a
happier time,
because that's all we want.

Introducing the new Renaissance

of Thought.

Think.

All those lies.
All that bullshit.
Just thoughts.

Think—
this medicine I take at bed
that swells my head with cloudy visions,
that fills me up with
dreams of the crest,
and even my own
death—
just thoughts.

Think...
about this poem—
about the reason I call myself
a poet.

I am just a thought—
a backgammon game
in your memory.

I am the first kiss and the last.
Tattooed with the number 3 on my back.

Think—
this is a funeral procession to a long weekend.

And after the wedding
of Tuesday through Thursday,
we are reborn on Friday,

only to return back to Earth on Monday.

And I only hope that you can do the same.

Think–
This is a tiny seed and
I am going to plant it.

Till I'm the only living thing,
the last angry poet on the planet.

The Last Angry Poet on the Planet

Come one, come all,

watch as I fall,
over my words, over religion,
over denial, over intuition,
over imagination, over hatred
and the realization–
that all this that I wrestle with,

all these thoughts–
are paper
villages.

All these loose-leaf poems are tombs
where my
life lives.

This is my womb.

This is a crumb of a piece of a pie,
one that gets smaller each time I try,
one that gets larger as my belly empties out.

This is my handle. This is my spout.
This is a fight over normal and not.

This is a thought, one that still walks, talks,
and like a moving clock,
ticks and tocks,
till time stops on my watch.

Tattoo 3:30 on my wrist.

That's when I know it's time to take my medicine:
an energy drink, a licorice stick,
perphenazine, lamotrigine,
benztropine to keep the side effects down–
Ativan, (lorazepam),
Abilify in the morning–
a quick regiment of meds that
keeps the calm storm
in storage.

And then emerges from a dark, dark circle,
a man so mean, he turns himself purple.
Presses record, strums the first words,
and out from the warmth, he becomes...

ManTheStorm.

JFK/U Mass

Out from the Warmth I Become

I hear thunder.

And soon the lightning will appear, strike twice
and feel warm, like the storm brewing inside
and at home.

If this spinning cycle
comes full circle,
it can't hurt you,
any more than your thoughts do.

Maybe it will be a warning,
that strange days are coming.
Maybe the life I'm livin', it's time for a change.
Cause the times they are a-changin',
and it's not the hurricane
that storms close,
it's the lack of love for yourself and
this city, I suppose.

I'm on the train again
at a standstill at UMass.
I can't let these feelings overwhelm me.

I see the trees blowing violent in the breeze.
Maybe it's my time to stop being blind.
And look at this world I forget to watch.
Maybe this is how I am supposed to see– reality.

To See- Reality

Let's all look.
The sky has gotten darker
and now I'm underground
listening to *Combat Rock*.

Joe Strummer singing about your three rights:

1. "Not to be killed. Unless it is done by a policeman, or
an aristocrat".
2. "The right to food money".
3. "The right to free speech (as long as you're not dumb
enough to actually try it)".

The reality, sadly, is rights aren't your reality.
Reality is really just a dream for people to believe that
there is reality.

Reality is controlled by love.
If you don't love then reality
turns angry and cold,
making your reality miserable
and you alone.

Reality can hit you on the head when you learn to speak
to the beauty with the blue dress,
but that is only a test
and you know you're both not ready yet.
And just like that she's gone.
Reality.

Continuous Reality

I see reality for what it is–
a brain-dead existence with a path to extinction.

We see pain all around us.
But when someone speaks up no one listens–
except the assassins.

See,
the third eye,
(the one located in your mind)
can create or destroy–

If we let that third eye open,
we learn that we can live without fear
of anything controlling us.

We can change our reality, but time is fleeting.

That's what I need to realize.
That my life
is only a minute of
a whole world's existence.

I must begin to realize that if I'm gone,
someone else will write like this, or similar to this.

Someone will act like me and talk like me,
and the 3 will change hands.

Oddball is my dream, has been since I was fifteen.
When I'm gone
I hope it exists in someone as strong.

You know what?
I can change the world.

Say it out loud to the crowd:
I can change the world.

Say it to each other:
We can change the world.

And begin to believe it.

I can change the world.

If you want it, it will come to you.

If you let it be true,
it will come to you.

My sympathies, you must have an allergy to reality.

ANDREW

Allergy to Reality

When I think like this, I start to breathe heavy.
My throat swells and I cough violently.
I guess in the end, I'm allergic to reality.

The reality that I could be burned to death,
or freeze to death, swim too far down
and lose my breath–

they call that
the bends.
It's when your lungs explode and you're done.
The end.

There are many ways to die, but only few ways to live.
The bright side is my own mind.
I feel like I am living
this reality till the abyss of mind, motion, and metal melt.

This is alright with me.
Living strange.

I don't think it would be the same, if I decided to change,
put the pen and paper away, call it a day.

I like the fact that if asked
I could pass a drug test and don't need the weed
that others need. I may drink, or drink a caffeine
laced drink, and then I start to think quick, and release
the grip
on each chord's fingertips.
Start singing a song, and let it go on.
Till I feel like it's done–

a happy thought that keeps me moving.

Listening to *Machine Gun Etiquette*
right now, and I feel good.

I feel like a new dollar bill, till it's used up like the water
in the well.
Like the diving bell that lets us know that we have stayed
too long and need to come up for air.

Flowing downstream and swimming back up,
and when the times get rough, at least
I still have a dollar and a dream.
Or a pen and a paper, a guitar and a pick, a girlfriend and
a kiss–
a life that isn't as bad as I think it is.

My blood flows
Celtic Green, and always in ink form.

Playing in each poem with my form,

like ManTheStorm, the world is only as real as you want
it to be.
So, enjoy this time, while we're all still free and
breathing.

Scream like hell to the sound of the division bell.

And that my friends is real speaking.
Enjoy the reading,
and let your freak flag fly, Boston.

Boston

The best place
in the world.

My home.

Exciting Night Tonight

Let's see where my brain takes me—
undertones, low and off key.

Making rhymes pop out of the ugly sunshine.
Yeah, it's the ugly sunshine that makes me feel sublime.

I'm an animal in the wild, running down
the drain into a secret space.
Where the neurons firing
start to sketch clear lines through my brain
and I can focus like window frames.
Where a record scratch repeats the chorus.

The pain goes away when the game is played and I'm all
in
from the beginning
to the end.

And, I'll be writing.
Fighting fear and riding lightning,
taking the crowd by storm,
rocking each stage that I step on.

Make you feel something.
Make you hear something.
Maybe learn something.

Grace on the Train

Hear the musicians play softly.
A lady sips tea, reading her book.

We see her, though she doesn't see herself quite yet.
She's never been respected, or loved quite right.

She lost her husband to a Cancer Call.
And now she sits quietly listening,
to the soft rhythm of the musicians.

Her son's in prison and she misses him.

Sipping her tea, I see her.
She seems like her name may be Grace.
The only softness she maintained
are the lines on her face,
above her brow,
too far from home, she wants to go home now.

Grace, won't you stay awhile and let us see your smile.

The music overwhelms her and she forgets
about her world.

I look up from my daydream already at
Downtown Crossing,
in the middle of Boston, and I feel awesome.
And I want Grace to feel the same.

I'm sure Grace is not her name.
She sits quietly on the train, not speaking to me,
or speaking at all.
I imagine her wondering when she can come home

and why life has to be so hard.

Her husband died in 2006.
Her son Jack was 18. Her daughter Lucy was 12.

The days were different after dad died.
They were darker.
Less light crept in.

Jack got caught up in the violence of a bitter bet, one that
couldn't be forgotten.
Lost in gunshots, his friend ended up in a coffin, and
Jack sits in prison still waiting for the warden.

As for Lucy, she always was smart, good in school,
varsity jacket on her shoulder...
but sometimes life takes over, and this time it wasn't
expected...

the drunk driver blindsided her with his brand-new
Lexus.

The rain starts falling hard, as the traffic stops;
as the ambulance approaches the broken glass; as the
medics surround Lucy.

Grace can hear sirens from the train,
and wonders when this rain will stop.

She doesn't know yet about Lucy
as she listens to the music,
when her phone
rings at Park Street.

While the sullen street performer sings sadly,

"You are my sunshine
my only sunshine…"

And she drops the phone
and weeps.

Listening to the music,
she hangs her head, and prays softly,

please don't take my sunshine away.

And Grace covers her head
and exits the train into the falling rain.

Trying to find peace in all her pain.

BROADWAY

New Ceremonies for Old Skin

See this old skin, see these baggy eyes, see this plastic smile and lions grin?

Let the ceremonies begin.

See this dragon walk? Breathe into a bastard's lung, see the wall of blue inching in?

Let the crest of the wave carry me home–
let this loser win.

Now let's dive into this spectacular display.

It's
a parade of misdirected saints,
all running the wrong way to the end of the race.

It's
a ceremony, all of us new,
wondering what we are supposed to do.

The wrench in my mind has unwound my
clock,

and has pushed me back to when I couldn't talk and I couldn't walk,

and couldn't hold a pen in my hand.

When I couldn't sleep, and collapsed on the bridge, back where I used to live.

Alone with a vaudeville tramp, living for something I
couldn't quite grasp.

Just a handful of scraps,
memories put into a loose-leaf binder,

where the welcome are unwelcome, we begin to rewind
here.

When the soul of a misfit was hung at the gallows and
darkness lifted,
and the sun stole our shadows–
brought us to a place the pen and misfit made.

A new ceremony for old skin, and the band it played,

on and on, and
                on and on.
Then Leonard
took the stage.

And that was the dream, and it reoccurs every night, and
goes away when I wake.

Taken away by the crest of a wave.

Leaving a memory,
in an
American
grave.

I am an American Ghost

I am a character.
Big head.
Balloon eyes.
Small legs.
Tiny shoes.

I am a character.
Big ears.
Big fears.
World traveled.
But still here.

I am a character.
A creature-feature.
No arms, no legs.
Haunting fields.
Knowing nothing.
Wondering why
I'm still here.

I am a character.
I kick and scream at
steel posts.
I let the stocks blister
my wrists.
I feel nothing.
I feel everything.
But I do not exist.

I am a character.
My eyes are blue and green.
My teeth are sharp.
I am a work of art.
I am the *Mona Lisa*.

I am a character.
I am high strung,
or strung out.
I see gentle waves
beneath my feet.

I run from science.
I am a scientist.

I run for war.
I am a pacifist.

I am a lie detector.
I lie the most.

I am the son
of the spirit
of the Holy Ghost.
I am syrupy sweet
like French toast.

I am an American.
I am an American ghost.
I am an American.
I am an American ghost.

Sober

Well of the world, it makes pearls stand up in the
sand–
needs comfort like sunshine to a plant.
It needs healing like a blistered hand,
from strumming the strings in a one-man band.

Well of the world, it drops down, and fills the soil with
water–
makes the love grow like a father to a daughter, from
a seed to a flower,
to an empire that lost all its power,
fighting itself hour to hour.

And back again, the hearts of men
fill up like sand in an hourglass,
and start to recede like the tide on the beach,

losing time we can't get back.

On *MURS For President*, MURS
says, that the trick in life,
is to keep your glass half full,
while keeping other's glasses full as well.
And when I try to do that,
I spill my glass.

So, I fill it up again with medicine, or the pen, and
try to make sense of the idea,
that we are all going to die, so, why do we waste time
with hate?
In a life that doesn't exist longer than a cold kiss?

And if we used all this energy,
we constantly crave–

what if we flipped our negativity to positivity?
How many lives could we save?

So much pain I see on these city streets.

People bleeding because someone sees them as strange,
so much pain,
so much pain.

People
reminiscing on a
city bench
about the happiness they had, and wondering
where it went.

People so far gone, they're impossible to reach.

And then there's me, a poet who sees it all
and records it all in
Oddball Magazine,
who tries to teach
but needs to find
where *his* love is, and how far gone is *his* mind,
and whether these words make sense
or are just a waste of time.

And on and on, the sober song writer sings softly,
and on and on, the sober song writer sings softly,
on and on, the sober song writer sings softly,
to the end of his song.

delete, destroy, and return to the world.

I'm going to calm down,
write a thought that has meaning now.

So, here I am, and lost as I've ever been–
I have two things to do: sleep or create.

I can't sleep because I slept too late,
so, I'm going to sit down and try to create.

Words can be beautiful when you let them
strike the heart with meaning.

Words can be ugly when you lose feeling,
and if your heart is still beating,

then you haven't lost feeling.

There is a lot of emotions up in the air.
Ask God, is he there, and you might feel something
there.
Ask the devil, and you know he's always there,
being the catalyst for destruction and despair.

I don't need anyone; I just need to find strength
in myself,
like my dad once told me,
put the helmet over my head, and say, protect
my thoughts
from leaking out like a leaky faucet.

But I know I have this little imp inside making me
noxious,

every time I clean out my closet,
he throws more shit on it.

But honestly, my health needs a booster shot;
thought I was strong enough, guess not.

But I have to find the strength.
It lies in me somewhere.

Bipolar is just another place,
and I've already been there.

And diagnosing me different–
I really don't care.

Cause we all have our own crosses to bear.

I'm strong enough, and just down in the
rough; trying to dig up enough stuff and
bury it deep down, I guess I should let it all out, cry on
your shoulder, but you know I'm not going to do that.

Because every day I get older,
I become more like a soldier–
an eagle-eye stare on a world grown colder,
and yeah, it's not over,
I know I'll get through this.

I'm tough enough to deal with this shit,
without turning it all to weakness.

Just have to pretend, that everything is ok again
and keep on with the peace, and keep on with

the pen.

Because I try to be who I am, when truth is I don't
know what I am, or where I've been, and why I
can't find my mind,
time to sleep again, but the world is Peace and Zen.

And if I look hard enough, something will tell me
that I'm more than just a psyche-ward-celebrity.

I have to keep it going, one foot after another.

Be real, stay real, and find something in nothing,
cause I know I have it in me,
to transcend through this negativity.
I've got to keep it in center,
the cypher the circle,

the whole in the half–
the 20/20 eyes I see through.

This is just a hurdle,
and you know I'm stronger than this–
kill the negativity, and let the poison
seep out of my skin,
collect it in a pan, and put it in the trash bin.

delete, destroy, and return to the world.

Make something out of this pain.

This world is yours.

Note to Self

Self,

keep your head up high,
when you feel so low,
cause the world is changing,
and time feels slow.

And you know it feels like
a vicious undertow.

But witness this–
the kid with
no help left, who puts slits in his wrists–
think of the cat, who got caught with a bag,
and is having problems with getting a job,
more than you have.

You? You're a college grad–you got more choices
than: You want fries with that?

Or think of the lady, who's just a baby,
who's having a baby, and keeps cutting class
to throw up in a bathroom stall, to bang
her head on the wall, cause her baby has no dad.

Think about that,
when you get down like this.
That your arms aren't broken,
and your mind is sane,
and there has to be a reason for all this pain.
Like Evidence said, pain leaves the body,
and there flows weakness with it.

So, keep legit kid, when you feel like this,

no one can hurt you more than you did.

You're the cat, who has stripes on his back—
a legit heart attack, that's waiting to be had.

Because hearts are going to stop
when they hear these thoughts.

Each poem I've wrote, each notebook I've written in.

A cat who is smart and intuitive—
you have to prove it to yourself kid.

That there's no one else in this world,
who has gotten through it and did it like this.

keep your head up, Self.

You're killin' em softly,

and the way I write,
I don't think anyone can stop me.

Fast to Say Finished

Please let me go away to another place.

Where the fire melts the fear away, and the warm water
flows blue and green, where the fat falls off the bone
makes a dream sing.

They say, under their breath, that this world you live in
and the way you live it, brings you closer to your death.

That the stomach expands and contracts, and the lungs,
pink now black, are coughing and growing sick from the
strength I lack, and the weakness I have.

I exist only in a minute, and soon I am fast to say I'm
finished. Throw the pen away; burn the book I'm
writing. And say this is the last poem; I'm sick of trying.

But I guess I'm fast to say I'm finished, and I know I
have to keep on,

strumming my guitar–
staring at the stars–
writing with my pen,

drunk in bars or to keep from sleeping on the train–
to keep staring at each person who looks at me
and notices the words Oddball and Magazine scribbled
on the front cover.

I guess I'm quick to say I'm finished and I'll never do this
again, but as long as I have a commute, you'll see me

writing on the train.
Scribing my name
on every, single, ugly, page.

SOUTH STATION

Can you save a sinner with a swear jar?

Look, we all see the world in two degrees.
One that sees the world as what it is–
what we think it should be.
Another part that seems more like
what I see, a world of prayer and profanity.

My dad tells me and Lisa agrees, that my poetry
is beautiful, but when I swear, it brings it down a notch.

Then I think, *well shouldn't all poetry be appreciated?*
And then I think about
Hip Hop.

I guess I went off my rocker, at the show the other night.
My friend Rob came up and said after the set,
 "damn man, you got to think of what you said."

I don't see it as a bad thing or a good thing.

But if I offend you, what should I do?
Why am I wasting time on this, defending what I do?

I know that I can write without it, but if what I write,
when I'm down, depressed, or up and lifted, if I cannot
read the words to you
as they are written–

fuck, then where's the freedom?

Still Some Time to Write

My train hasn't quite stopped.
Not at my destination, or my train of thought.
Keeping in check my ego, let it go.
This style I have comes from endless practice.
I used to write during the teacher's lessons
and poems on the back of vocab tests.

Even on my PSATs and SATs I got bored, wrote a
poem, and drew an *Oddball* 3.

When times got rough, and my family split up,
I found this love.
And now I have it down to a science.

This love I have, to put down thoughts in between blue
lines and white spaces, shapes us.
Not just me reading this, but you hearing this.
Let the love release us. And get down to the sound
of voices speaking from the heart, cause that's what
poetry is all about.
I think I am beginning to figure that out.
Or maybe it's not for you.
Try to find an outlet freer than poetry.
All you need is a pen and a pad,
or a street,
or a wall.

Writing when we're down, we all do; we all feel low.
That's when we flow, poets and prose.
We all saved ourselves from the undertow.
At least I did.

Learned at a young age that I can do this.

So, when Mom and Dad called it quits, people died
and illness set in, when I had no girlfriend, and no
money in my wallet,
when me and my friends were alcoholics, using toxins to
alleviate the pain in my brain...
poetry got me through the day.

I prayed.
God gave me the test,
either change your life, or die like the rest.

So, I started listening to DASEFX and A Tribe Called
Quest,
started reading Kerouac and the lyrics of Cohen, and
there I was
a fuck-up, but I found love,
in this thing I can't give up.

It's called poetry.

But to me, I call it therapy, and something that saved me.

Start Strong Finish Strong

It's about starting strong
and finishing strong–
that's the lifeline.
The main train I write on,
moves on and my music is gone.
So, I let the day wash over my shoulders,
let the night fuel me for tomorrow.
And without warning,
the train stops and soon I am walking.

I see the trees with the green leaves.

I see a man waving peace.

I see three children in the streets,
playing.

I see a future for all of us,
and it makes me feel good.

I see a weakening wind as it rushes back into my lungs.

I see a world with no guns.
I see people flying free.

Being the people, the individuals they should be.

I see the waves of water, ebbing back and forth.
I see a world listening to each other's every word.
I see no barriers between us.
I see fireworks lighting, in the distance.
If I look hard enough; I can even see me in them.

I see no blank stares.
No violence.

Just writers and dancers,
jumping in puddles, in rainstorms.

I see music being made in the cellular form
I see a world that is not blind.
Isn't cold but not warm—
something between a baby's first step
and a blind man's vision.

I see a single cell organism,
making something out of nothing.
I see God's warm hand, and I see a purple flower.
I see dreams of subways, and concrete bridges.
I see an ivory tower.
I see castles in the distance.
Is this what heaven is?
I see a world finally accepting me,
and seeing truth in this illness.
I see a poet's brilliance, a beautiful rainbow.
An undertow that's resilient, watching the ebb and flow.

And me
receding
back to the train, the stares, the shame,
the idiot job, the reasons why I am writing,

and I'm back, alone again
with people who don't know me.

And this poem—
just a dream from
a steam-powered brain,
on a slow-moving train.

Finishing to stop these thoughts.
Then the pen stops.

I put a signature and a 3 on the page,

and it all goes back to nothing.

No beautiful beach,

just a train
full of
people–

people who don't know me,

watching the freak
write his poetry.

Same Damn Train Poem

Well here I am again.
Must be 5 pm again.
Same damn train.
Same damn distance.
Same damn sentences,
locked into rhythm.
Same damn pen.
Same damn people.
Same damn feeling
of mediocrity and never
quite equal.
Same damn hands,
shaking with energy–
this is what my pills
do to me.
Same old shirt.
Same old tie.
Same old holes in my shoes.
Same damn papers people
holding in front of their face.
Same damn space
with someone's crotch
in my face.
Some business man moves, and
I can breathe again.
Same damn Tuesday evening.
Same damn therapy session.
Same Sense One
ranting and raving.
Same pain.
Same gut feeling.
Same headphones,
playing songs that either
put me together

or make me feel alone.
Soon I'll be home.
Same old story.
3-story apartment.
No dog barking.
Dirty carpet.
Dishes and laundry.

At least I get to see Lisa
put her arms around me.

Heat Wave

Every evening about this time,
I start to lose my mind,
so, I start to rhyme
to pass the time.

But today something is wrong.
Not only is my mind unglued,
but the heat on this train,
is like 102.
And it was cold before,
and I can do with that usually.
But man, I'm fat and have a jacket on,
and feel like I'm baking with no AC.

This actually reminds me
of a commercial
I saw on TV,
about a train breaking down
starting to steam.
And all of a sudden, the steam
turns to a cold breeze,
and out comes the Bermuda shorts
and bikinis, and beer flowing free,
and people start to *party*.

If I look around this train,
I don't see a *party*.

And I wish it was cold–
so cold it could snow.

The breeze outside is nice,
but damn it's hot in here.
And I could use a cold beer–

and a bath to break this fever.

And I don't feel right at all.
No, I don't feel right at all,

But man, I can't fall.
No man, I can't fall.

I can't fall

When I feel like this,
the ignorance turns to bliss.
I'll ignore the constant fight
inside my mind.
I'll embrace the pain,
stay calm on this train.
Started a change in medication,
began to kick in this morning
at the bus station.
Nervous energy,
no empty spacing.
Playing each note off key, and
pulled CSRs and started placing.
I pulled about a hundred disconnects
before coffee time and lunch break.
Then I went on to place
conversions,
and oh, the anguish when you get it
perfect, and it gets rejected.

Like building a house, and then
having it torn down because of faulty construction.
A stupid liquid language of numbers
that equal the sum of 9 digits
and mechanical functions–
needless algebraic language.

But really, this telephony
is Greek to me, using clichés and hyperbole, and rhymes
to complain about my day, when in reality

telephony is ruining my life.

Blank Spaces

I see blank spaces; blue lines like bus lines, to move the
words slowly down the line.

I feel like I need to fill them in with words in rhythm.

My notebook becomes a prison for each consonant and
lyrical syllable. Each vowel gets played–
put in line, and then I close the book for about 8 hours
time.

And I open it again with new rhymes to push and fight to
get some sunlight.

Many of my words are locked away in solitary in my
library.

Sometimes, they get visits from the poet with the
headphones, writing his poems,
looking back at the ones he has done.

When this happens, some words get conjugal visits, with
witnesses, usually crowds and therapists.

I let them stream out of the page, speak, and let them
have their day on stage.

And if I really like the words,
they get life, and grow with me, while some poems find
homes; some get cobwebs on them,

and need revisiting, because every word's a prisoner–

and every prisoner has a story.

DOWNTOWN CROSSING

Feel Like Peace

Feel like
(a)
piece

of
shit.

Cause you make me feel like this.

My mind is a slave ship. All my feelings, emotions, and thoughts are locked.

Sometimes, I would rather turn the lights off.
Go to sleep; never leave my bed.

Maybe you think I am a joke, but I'm the realest there's ever been.

I must unlock the demons, let them all out.
Hope you're not squeamish princess, but a piece of shit cannot live like this.

When I'm all alone, and not around the people on this train, the thoughts stop.

So, what's real?

You know what? Fuck You!
That's what's real.

I'm sick of playing it cool.
How about you?

You want to judge, when you do nothing to help anyone?

You want me to write about love, then give me some.

All I hear every day is ridicule. Every goddamn day!

Talking shit about me cause I look nervous and don't walk your way.

I don't need the world of joint smugglers.
Where you question your friends,

like, "why did you say that to me, I thought you'd understand?"

I thought talking to you would make me feel better.
You know what don't bother.

I don't read the religious trash you spew in your pews.
You want to be a true person?
Realize there's a million people different then you.
No worse, no better–
just because they don't know the bible by the goddamn letter.

I'm fine, don't worry about me
I'll keep my mind locked in slavery.
Letting every piece of shit who says something to me, get to me.
You know what, this is what you want me to be…then fine
I'll let it be.

Let it be.
Like the dead Beatles.

Train Poem # 710

710 thought broadcasts today.
710 negative thoughts to normal situations.

At least a hundred in the morning at the train station,
and depression is driving my train of thought right out of
rotation.

And now I'm back and blind.
Trying to unwind after the grind.
My spine is tired of holding my pathetic head up.

I feel like I'm in cement.
Demented and stuck.
My mentality ferments in a cold basement where no light
comes in to illuminate the empty spaces.

So how was *your* day?

Did you feel love today?

I wish you do.

I hope you have not only a good weekend, but a nice life.

Where you don't feel too beaten
and don't feel too stuck,
I hope you never feel this defeated.

I hope you're strong enough to rise above.
I hope and wish you all the best of luck and the lonely
find love, and the sad get hugs.

I hope if you don't have a lot of money, that you find a
lucky lottery ticket and if you hate your job, you quit.

I hope that if you're tired
you sleep well again.
I hope you can still read these words
that are written. I hope you can still dream and your
dreams are vivid–
that your life is vivid.

I hope you and your wife are happy.
I hope that your husband treats you good.

I hope if you're as lost as I am, you are one day
understood.

I just wish you all the best and hope I can feel like you
once or twice. I hope your happy and healthy, I wish you
all the best in life.

That's what I would love, to feel like the rest, instead of
drowning in a world that really never relents.
Never lets up until your dead.
I want peace of mind, like a man who finds the stone that
gives him the ultimate prize.
I wish you could see the world through my eyes.
I wish my mind would be silent, and I wore those rose-
colored glasses that you do.

I wish I could sleep forever and dream like someone does
who's deep in love.

I just wish this train ride was over,
so I could put this pen down.

Put (This Pen) Down

Pick it up, the pen
in your hand, look at it.
Put it to the edge of the margin.
Now let's begin.

See, I make music, melodies on any whim.
You think your liquor is quicker–

your liquid thinking?
Drops of water.

In a minute,
I'll show you who's timid, when I open the doors of this
train and start break dancing on the engine.

I'll light a fire in your kitchen.
Set fire to your system.

Pick up the pen and let the ink spill out and inspire.

Rewire your programming, that nasty dance of no.
Bring it to a boil, open up the time capsule and let your
soul explode.
That's what I'm talking about.
Let the chaos inside out and put it down
in a poem.

And to each and every witness–
you know how the story goes.

Spinal Chords

I think my mind is about to go nuclear.

I should grab a cylinder and paint my name on the train
with my own personal VIN number.

So, today...
So, today's the first day of summer.
Let it all hang out.
Let loose and feel proud.
Make some noise, let me hear the crowd.

Let me hear the disillusioned feel something
other than their bruises.
Let me feel the immense relief, the powder keg release

of a million matches being lit.
Watch the sparks light up the night.

And in the torrid night, somewhere in the deep of the
ocean,

a big fish is chasing a small fish when 10 small schools of
fish grab the big fish and tear him limb from limb.

I call that a revolution.

Downtown Crossing

The bowl of oranges that surrounds us, is just a bowl of oranges.

And though my degree from UMASS grows dust on my mantle,

I think I got the program, or I'll get with the program.

My hands are white knuckled
from riding in this space shuttle,
no room for oxygen,
so, I place my feet into my moon suit,
and surf the silver sky on my moon boots.

You always told me I could escape reality by letting my dreams play out.

But we're only at
Downtown Crossing.
7 stops left with 10% battery.

Listening to the boom-bap
to try and drone out the laugh track.
Sit back and try and relax
and watch the train
go off the train tracks.
God, I want my mind back.

Birdcage

7:00, I worked overtime.
Now I'm at Park.

My eyes blink slow.
The train moves fast trying to make the energy overlap,
and soon sunshine,
and the Boston Skyline.
Beautiful and vivid, like a picture of a flower.

Like a badge of honor, I wear this three on my back and
shamrock on my hat.

Damn, the Pru looks beautiful tonight, all lit up.
The boats sail the Charles, and I wish you were here to
see it, Melody.

I wish you could calm down your mania, and let your
dreams invigorate and regenerate, like leaves on a peach
tree.

But Melody, you still live in your bird's cage.
You still dream a prince will take you away.

You still think there's an island to escape to, and you're
an island, so the island is you.

To those I've lost, I miss all of you.

The calming sound of the revving train brings me back to
Boston.

And a plane and a train ride away, Melody sings softly in
her birdcage, watching the rain, waiting for the time
when her door will open.

PARK STREET

The Rain Dance

Man, the sun is hot today.
Good to be on the train and in the shade.

I have the A.C. in me calming quietly over the literature I
read.

All I need is a pen and a notebook and everywhere I look
begins to change–

a poem into a painting,
a blank canvas into brilliance.

All I hear is the gentle sound of a scratching pen, on a
blue lined page.

They say with age, we start to become complacent, but
my brain is strange and will never stay patient.

Unless the meds inside start to subside, and Mania
becomes too strong, I'll stay working, writing poems and
songs.

I am an iron man, an iron brain.
I am the only life on this train.
I am the nucleus, of an atom you can't fathom.

I am a stranger with a strong soul, never to be sold,
rusted but still gold, still walking the line of demon and
divine.

This rain dance we dance together, soothes the
weathered brain, ready to stand up and transform.

Never stay the same, this I can teach you.
A million can sing, but only a few will reach you.

And like Brother Ali, I sing these songs of peace on the
city streets.

One day the beauty will meet the beast,
and the sun will swallow all the feast.

The sheep will keep listening to their beats, but only few
will see the real emcees–
poets with poems, real poetry.

What happened to the art of war, of words on paper, and
spray can vapor?

What happened to the words people speak making others
feel free?–
That's why I love Brother Ali.

His songs are swimming through my headphones, and all
of a sudden, I'm in a crowded room and someone hands
me a microphone.

A poet's energy, and some rude, rude, beats–
that's all I need.

Now, I'm at South Station,
and the drums in my headphones
have begun to
gather clouds.

Clouded

Rhymes like Rubik's Cubes, complex
like Kubrick movies.
Mash it up like Monster man.
Just me and the drumbeat, beating on the trashcan.
Light up the hash in your coat, clouded–
control the codes, build those binary blocks.
Cluster flies fly the friendly skies, and I am wasting time
on a train with traffic. This rhythm, this writing, terrific
magic.

ManTheStorm making the ladies swoon, making
mommies cry, kissing babies, cutting ribbons at
supermarkets, spouting campaign promises–President-
elect-the-storm.
Man, I wish I was anywhere but here.

Fear gathering faster with each added commuter, and
now we're at Porter.
Push on soldier, the fight is almost over.
Alright enough alliteration,
all is alright,
in this world of imagination.
Got to say peace, draw a 3, and sign the sheet.

And off exits the poet
at Davis Square Station.

A Rock or a Stone

Priceless artifacts of pain–
what makes me more qualified to write about pain?
Pain's my life.

Afraid of the water, but not afraid to drown.

If you save me from the weather, we're all better off
together, but around this town, I'll still be alone–
a clod or a clown, a rock or a stone.

You pitch me into the deep, to sing for the sheep I eat for
supper.
Poetry, my lover, the unity of pens and palettes.

In the world of green, I am just a spec in the mirror, a
kink in the machine.

A leaf on a tree, but trees die.

But not poetry.
It lives on in every poem and every song.

Words live on (in every poem and in every song)

Poetry flows through me like too much coffee.

I'm going to try and write a song now.

Like Minor Threat, at least I'm trying, what the fuck have you done?

See, I see people walking around and, in my mind, they walk over me like cement.

But I am trying to represent this illness in packed pavilions, losing myself over the words written.

I keep it on for the millions.
Call me an advocate for anyone ever called faggot.

Now it's crowded, and my thoughts are getting louder, listening to Little Brother, listening to 9th makes everything better.
But now I too wonder. But inside I got the answer.

Get me a MPC and a beat conductor,
and like Dilla I will show you who is in this muthafucka.

Cold Freeze

I'm not ready to rock steady beats.

I'm out of this cold freeze.
So, I'll slow down and make Sense
make sense, and if I can do that
then I can make sense of myself.
Because Sense is the name written on the trains in Boston
outbound.
Tagged in subway stations.
Listed in the dictionary as logic of science.
And that's what I do, make sense of the life and bullshit I
put myself through.
Make sense of the world that hates me. The one I see
through.

Make sense of the world of $'s and cents. Because Sense
makes cents.
But Sense represents being a monster-poet-rhymer, self-
hater, promoter, long-time-lover, walking around static,
flagrant and flaccid, fluorescent and hell-bent on making
sense, when Sense is the only sense, that Sense ever
made.

and it's all
just a dream,
just a writer on a train—

and his re-run mind.

And in this re-run mind, I've died a thousand times and
one day you can write on my grave stone:

lived alone, died alone,
and bury me with a microphone.

Oddball Brain Damage

Yeah, that's what it is Brain Damage.
A rerouted, rewired brain, saying hateful shit, when I
really just want a sandwich.

Thinking obscene, unless I'm dreaming,
then things make sense to me and I want to keep
sleeping.

A heavy-breathing-demon, a songster-poet-madman,

a world that pushed me away long ago, a world that I
don't understand, and that doesn't understand me.

I see.
I fall into a pigeonhole, a world-wide-web-slinging
asshole. A foul-mouthed, bad tempered idiot,

I lose myself in my illness.

I ask for forgiveness from the princes and the princesses
that litter this city.

Maybe, I'm singing my own head to sleep, but really this
illness runs deep.

Hurts like a gash on my forehead, hurts like I am beaten
and broken, but not dead.

At least I have the power of words, to get over this hurt,
and get over this earth.

Where I was switched at birth, cursed to live like an
amputee,

yet my hands work freely, it's just my mind is no longer
with me.

I cannot control the hideousness of this silliness, just
trying to live my life without wishes or forgiveness.

Because I live like this.
But God made me like this,
and he gave me two wrists to make limp, or make fists–
take your pick princess.

Somerville

Sitting in a Somerville chair.

At *Sunshine Lucy's*, put up an *Oddball Magazine* flier. Started hanging out with the owners.

Listening to the Clash, and now Manu Chau,

sitting in a Somerville chair.

At *Sunshine Lucy's*

Where the Clash records play
And art grows and thrives.

Somerville, I love you.

Malaise

Went to the beach.
Went to a movie.
Went to bed; let the waves soothe me.

Walked down to the shoreline, and now I wonder, what have I done with this endless summer?

Apparently, I cut my feet among the sand, apparently, I have caffeine in the head, and pen in my hand.

But if everything is perfect in these Salad Days, why do I feel such a malaise?

Like my life is a train and I am a passenger waiting for the next stop.

I need to find hope, because the medication is not working.

I went to a movie; my mind ruined the whole thing.

I wish I could feel something other than sickness.

The chill of the summer breeze makes my fingers cold. And the warmth I had, just turned and froze.

Like this is it. Someday I suppose, I'll get out of this slump, maybe I will feel something other than numb. Maybe just maybe I'll become someone.

Bipolar is an animal. So is schizoaffective. It's basically medicating you down to keep you attentive, with no direction, and mild sedatives to keep you smiling and breathing.

I haven't slept well–
I think I'm still dreaming.

And if life is a 24-hour day, it's getting late in the evening,

and that's the story, no rhyme no reason.

CHARLES/MGH

Just Defeat

Just defeat the illness in me.
Just defeat this ill mentality.
Just defeat this mental slavery.
Just defeat it; don't let it defeat me.
Let each steady beat freeze the sheet
of paper, the loose-leaf page
to let me tell my story,
to let freedom out of my cage.
In a simple word, it is not a simple world.
It is a heart that keeps beating
as fast as a humming bird, and slowly as dirt.
It is a lowered line with a fish on a hook.
It is two story buildings,
or two stories from a crook.
It is the feeling of madness that recreates my past
each time I think back.
It's the useless love for drugs
that my friends all have.
It is a cemetery flower; it is a country grave.
It is the protesters,
and the pundits fighting over the earth.
It is just black ink, on a white lined page.

(It is a poet with mental illness, trying
to cope on this fucking train).

The Election (on we march)

Today elect me
into your society
of speed freaks,
and new-sneaker-sneaks
of poet-of-the-weeks
of jelly-of-the-month-
Ohio steaks.
Let me be your rhythm-push-pop.
Lick a world till it rusts, and don't stop.
Let me fly in a minute, and soon
I'll be finished.
Let me be the gas that goes to the engine.

Let me in. Elect me.

Like electricity to electricians,
madness to manics.
Elect me. Let me in.

Let me in,
like your next best friend.
Save me like a dog on a commercial.
Let me be controversial.
Let me be your surgeon.
Let me be your red cells.
Let me be your Amoeba—
a music shop where the
party don't stop.
Let me be the bowl, the bong.
Light me up, and let the smoke talk.
Let me be the dead,

that resurrects every Halloween's end.
Let me be your dinosaur, and you
can find my artifacts.
Take a step back
and relax.
Elect a liar to the lion's mouth.
Elect a mountain to the aftermath.
Elect a stronger man than me.
Let me be the reason that you rhyme.
Let me be Sublime in 95,
going back to a happier time.
Let me be, or let me in to the secret society
you live in.
Because I have blinders on, and a liar's grin.
I just want to be you.
Let me in, dog. Let me in.

Let Me In

It's hot out today.
Good to be on the train
with the A.C.
Good to be able
to move freely.
Crazy with no psych wards holding me.
No white chords, no vest
where your arms rest
in a restless state, like mania
or hypomania.
A world of insanity seems sane,
but no one knows me on this train.
This vehicle.
This theatrical production of
buttering bread.
To feed your family.
To listen closely
to the horse's hooves.
To see everything
that moves.
To be a rude boy
in the streets.
To be waving threes to find peace.
Not white sheets.
Not toe tags
on dead feet.
A world where
a warrior of words
can live with a
warrior of weapons.
Use my words like armor.
Use my words to plant
me when I'm too far off the ground,

too high to stand up,
and sense to know when to back down.

And courage
to never sit down
until it's my turn
to drive the bus.

Let me in.
Ride with me.

Ride (with us)

With us you can't lose.
Dude on the train
has a ukulele and hemp shoes.

James Brown in my ears,
and I feel good, with my bad self.
Under control, meds off the shelf.

Met a beautiful me today,
and I love it to death.

A pen got a funeral coming
but this one will get through
to the end of this page.
To the end of the train ride,
to the end of this stage.

I could see myself
lying in a casket
buried with pens—
disappear like magic.
Come back made of magnets.
And light up the whole planet.
Watch the light
shift on the train walls
and we still remain
Oddballs,
but who fails and who falls?
And who comes real with it?
I'm not finished.
Who can stand,
and sit with this sickness?
Make sense of something

unseen
and put it all together into
—neon lines
—lightsabers
—stars that vibrate
—shoes that disintegrate while we walk.

Our hands they clasp together
as we journey this planet together.

In hell or in heaven
there will always be angels.
And there will always be an end
to a beginning.
Only to begin a new beginning.
and Bam!
Like that next stop,

Davis Square
Train Station.

Listening to Cursive

Another hell-bent day
on a train that takes me away
from work,
but not away from my pain.
Tonight is rehearsal,
where poets will make love
to the music.
Where everything in the world
will seem perfect.
Until I'm off the stage
and out in the rain,
in a rainy-day jacket–
in a famous blue rain coat.

Leonard would be proud
of me today
I mention his name and
I think I feel the same.
Because I straight rocked the stage.
Because the situations I deal with;
he dealt with–
with melody and harmony.
And the only weapon God gave
me to get through daily
is poetry and a large vocabulary–
which is alright with me so far.

My friend Tuck called me
a *wordsmith*.

It made me
feel something again,
other than depression,

madness,

and movement.

I Will Be True To This Game To The End

Seriously, ManTheStorm what's your function?
To make music and put words together, then do nothing?
To move around, pivoting in a world that is too numb?
To feel something, to write your pain down, record it,
and perform it with drums?

I am an uncaged animal on the stage.
Maybe that's the cards that I play with, this leather,
weathered face.

Maybe someday I will see the blue,
like it's an ocean, not just the lines I write on
and the feelings I go through.
Maybe.
Maybe, I'll let these feelings in me flow freely.
Because Love and Longing, makes for good poetry.

I really wish I wasn't here right now.

And there is still so far to go to get home.
And here I am, reappearing as a freak in
my mirror.
Slowing down, feeling my fear, letting
the right rhythms into this soulful system.
Listening to some soulful Soul Position.
I just want to feel like I'm winning, not losing.
I feel low, down, sick, and stupid.
The smile I wear, it matches my shoes.
Three lines down the center, with atmospheric
symmetry.
With nothing to prove, there's nothing left to lose.

When your lost in a world of twos,
there's no room for a 3 in this world.

Something like a Dream

Today, I will melt
In the 100 and 3 degree
weather.

Today, I will break down
this puzzle, and put it
all together.

Today, I fight for what my name is…
Today, I am the realest, and I feel like this.
Like I'm the truest poet to ever live.
Because I live this shit.
And survive it…

Some can live…
Some get by…
Some try too hard to fly
but fill their head with drugs
and mis-step,
like stepping and slipping
on the train tracks,
you realize that this is it.

One slip, you're finished.
There is only one life I know of.
So, fuck all the other stuff
and fill your heart with love.

And maybe we will meet some day by some dumb luck,
and I will give you a poem, and you will give me a hug.

And I will say that I wrote this poem for you, and glad that you read my book. And beauty is only skin deep, sometimes you need to take a closer look.

And maybe you will see the scars on my arms are far lesser than yours, and that is because I was given this gift to write these rhymes.

I use my pen as a sword, to kill the negativity.
Refill me when this world has gotten too much for me.

And yeah, I have to take medications.
And yeah, I might be different,

but this gift that God gave me is the reason I am still living.

And the ink isn't drying, before the next page is written.

Jason in 2012

Jason Wright is the author of *A Letter to the World*. He is a tireless mental health advocate and public speaker. He is the editor and founder of *Oddball Magazine*, and co-host of the *Oddball Show Podcast*. He refuses to fall, is a champion, and your new favorite writer.

Special Thanks to...

I would like to thank my beautiful wife Lisa for believing
in me for all these years. To all my family and friends, I
love you all. Thank You Chad for what you do for
Oddball Magazine. Thank You Prof for what you do for
the *Oddball Show*. Thank You T.J. for our friendship and
for your help with this book. Thank You Andrew, Andy,
Adelon, and Nick for your friendship and guidance along
the way. Thank You Rob, for your friendship and
helping me with *Nevertown*. This project has been years
in the making and I am so grateful to everyone who has
helped me, has taken a look at it, or given me feedback.
To the friends I have had and the friends I still have,
please know I am grateful. And to the people who are
reading this on the train, the people who are reading this
with no hope, who may be far from home, do know I
have your back...and it will get better.

With Love,

Jason Wright

Made in the USA
Columbia, SC
12 January 2020